Lake Oswego Public Library
706 Fourth Street
Lake Oswego, Oregon 97034

All the Messiahs Agree

65093429

All the Messiahs Agree

David John Schleich

Crusoe House
USA: Portland, Oregon
Canada: Vancouver, British Columbia

©2017 by David John Schleich

All rights reserved.

This book, or parts thereof, may not be reproduced in any form without permission, except in the case of brief quotations embodied in critical articles and reviews.

Text and cover design by Richard Stodart

Cover and frontis:
Floating Through His Shape by Richard Stodart

ISBN: 978-0-9996233-0-5 Hardcover
Library of Congress Control Number: 2017960516

Printed in the United States of America.

Crusoe House
USA: Portland, Oregon
Canada: Vancouver, British Columbia

crusoehouse@gmail.com

contents

kodak haiku 9
a tine caught my heart 11
the recognition 13
the laving and the kissing 15
making for the temple 17
Crusoe waiting 19
new cruel green 21
just out of reach 23
the grace of lovers 25
dune woman 27
all the messiahs agree 29
holding hands in broad daylight 31
the sulphur priest 33
when they lie down 35
the terms of his surrender 37
sad proscenium 39
the name of the beloved 41
today I died 43
testament in rock 45
eggs in a nest 47
the perfect courtesy of water 49
fleeing to Catalonia 51
making for the beginning 53
the longing has no proprietor 55
the petrel and the fletcher 57

about the author 59

> April is the cruellest month, breeding
> Lilacs out of the dead land, mixing
> Memory and desire, stirring
> Dull roots with spring rain.
> T.S. Eliot, *The Wasteland*

> Whan that aprill with his shoures soote
> The droghte of march hath perced to the roote,
> And bathed every veyne in swich licour,
> Of which vertu engendered is the flour;
> Whan zephirus eek with his sweete breeth
> Inspired hath in every holt and heeth
> Tendre croppes, and the Yonge sonne
> Hath in the ram his halve cours yronne
> Geoffrey Chaucer, *Prologue to the Canterbury Tales*

> What is the late November doing
> With the disturbance of the spring
> T. S. Eliot, *East Coker II*

> Rise up, my love, my fair one, and come away.
> For, lo, the winter is past, the rain is over and gone;
> The flowers appear on the earth;
> The time of the singing of birds is come,
> and the voice of the turtle-dove is heard in our land.
> *Song of Songs*

9 **kodak haiku**

eyes thighs lips
in my mind each day
like breathing

a tine caught my heart

she snags my malaise with one swipe of blue eyes
flings it over her shoulder at the waiting women
she shows me cavalierly now
what I needed then

the sudden slash draws blood and quick cruor
saves everything

later the night becomes intolerable without her
until finally she appears
dowsing my heresy
you are the last of your kind, she says
save yourself from your own doom-rimed mouth
for some feelings are reached
only through poetry
or skin on skin

every sonnet in me shuts tight
until the idea of her is taut in my heart
like a possible canvas

finally, I pick up a wetted brush
to start

the recognition

they happened on a language
billowing, familiar
and from that moment memorized each other
and in every word that tasted of hearts on fire
they recognized the embedded etymology
of love that is not sin

all night her name was smooth and music
in his mouth its shape round and familiar
its letters lavender
its sound sloping to the diminutive

her perfect lips and the folding skirts of the rich earth
promised the memory of touch
spring warm seduced every splintered puddle
and the idea of the other
snapped open

touched to the core they were
by their first sudden breath grabbing kiss
and entering heat

persisting winter, bark-rough
could not slow the unravelling ice and white
the casting out of bloated facts
long locked and tough

spring love sharpened their hearts instead
for the sweet long work of love ahead

the laving and the kissing

she was startled
by the kind laving of her arm
he bathed her in thin sweet sap from early maples
he laid his cheek against her bare shoulder
beginning the ritual, the truth of flesh
and smooth convergence at her breast
she insinuated the cold arches of her tiny feet
into the soft warm curves behind his knee
searching for a night's berth
his legs were a grave
her lips soft spades

making for the temple

deep in the dark green wood
lured from lairs back in, well hidden
big cats watch vines circle the lovers' arms and legs
and witness ancient conundrums of love beginning

the lovers shed their city clothes
pad quickly through the friable understory
making for the temple
where other narrow eyes
will study every fluid move

another black panther comes
she is invisible, she is new
she slides alongside, follows
like a pilgrim in heat
she guards the passing lovers too

Crusoe waiting

fifty sea-nymphe Nereides reply suddenly
from their grotto at the bottom of the whirled sea
with you

and thus soothe again the vexed infinite ache of men
who have crossed wide water with the petrel
to where the sea licks the sand
and indifferent cerulean waves
bathe the naked feet of absent loves

my soul is coaxed to higher ground
your arrival propels me immediately
to stake this spot where you can do to me without apology
what rare rain evokes in the brown desert

that you found me on this vast littoral
accumulates into dense mystery
dares disturb the universe
though we leave no scar at all

how miraculous your form
exactly the way I love the feminine
no small matter, my Itaua woman
we submit to a destiny of inevitable long kisses
and understand as one clenched soul
this geography of tense and person

I have so many stories for you, my rose-cheek'd lover
adrift in lonely latitudes
we are now far enough from the shaping line of earth and water
to kiss urgently, again, again

the storm conjured by Eostre flung us here
this wild coast is where we learn
why your smile is my heart's home

later your eyes weep under the fierce sun
it's not the sun, you said

new cruel green

not once did his heart hesitate to meet
the impossible heat of her kiss
did he not hold her firm and long, just inside the loft
away from the order and the stir
of witnesses on the street

not once did they not obey the fierce code of lips
their bodies trembling beneath the towers of this new order
and where they did not think they would love again
suddenly weeks of love in hours

at dawn he implored the deaf world for redemption
save me from her beauty, he cried
he knew they heard everything
before there were words for their ears
or lunt to light a way from here

and when he asked later
about this new ballad of touch
she asked back
just at the moment when their desire
descended momentarily to grief
what is the good of love
in the cruellest month?

they traced the answer between them

fingers arcing, hers, then his
touching brave, tiny benediction blue lungwort
then they knelt before Eostre
remembering again her fragile power
and her impending splendid green

just out of reach

the imprint of her touch persists
covers his body with pools of her
elusive, stark
then the precise and wonderful memory arrives
like an arrow from her eastern shelter
and the kiss tipped head finds its mark

murmur of fenced passion blurs and nears
for what makes him man and shows him what is knowable
are her eyes, her kiss, her tears

he cannot discern the joker at work across a continent
yet knows he needs the whole strength of her body
braced and locked and learned all over him
and that undulating sadness
is but a carved instant in the medium of air

red eastern birds blissed on spring
thread throwaway paths in her yard
demonstrating forbidden morning lineaments
for tracing her breasts, her lips, her thighs
just out of reach

the grace of lovers

the grace of lovers slides up my spine tonight
so weary at three a.m. am I
recalling how her voice coaxed variegated birds
from their cotes in the spring just gone
she filled the air with butterflies
her flicking fingers and swerving palms
danced for me like an absent essence
filling my room with Babylon

I fear my body may will her here
momentarily
so I rise, go deeper into my sanctuary
where wild grapes encircle the idea of us
where crows came earlier to deliberate
to find the peace of creatures who do not hesitate
whose only forethought is contained in instants

above me the intelligent confusion of stars
like her face
is not there

In this moment, absent her
the grace of the world embraces, teaches patience
for life is not done with us, she said

earlier, the raw scream of the last late crow
ripped the sky's greying caul again

dune woman

dunegrass sentinels spread the word
she is walking north through sweet gale and sedge
in search of him this day
headed to bare sand hummocks bounded by morning glory
her head is down against the wind and spray
feet quick, not careless, crushing culm as she moves
toward flat-floored blowouts, and beachheads of new grass

she finds a flat ventifact where she sits
watching long grey waves pulsing in
each swash disturbing mirror bits of tiny suns
setting fire to testimonies of the unrequited

the air he breathes he knows is also breathed by her
their holy forms brace against the sea
the wind stings their eyes and their endless looking

he loves, she loves, it is enough
they are right here, they can hear the ocean
doing what it does

all the Messiahs agree

all the Messiahs agree
each time his hand feels her absence on the bed
he could not love her German eyes the more
nor when she looks up from her panting gut
and listens to their breathing

all the Messiahs agree
that her lips and his
sip desire like hummingbirds
he kisses her open mouth
while they lie on the plain bed
eating all the cake they brought
for the celebration

later it rains and guardian angels appear
washing them clean, reminding them to hide anything
which can comfort the enemy camp

he asks her to dance
under the blurred halo of the alley lamp
she asks him to grow spring wings with her
and lose their minds

instead they stay and read *Karenina*
he whispers the birthday song he wrote
and for a moment the verses change the skies

but then their minds pour poison which they drink
lassoing their naked arms, closing down their eyes

they send back to the sun
the spring buds of future flowers
and tell each other their histories

they give their hearts outright
to silence the eidolons an hour

like improvident tapers in blue wind
they wait for the times to change
until elusive taunts hiss from outside the pane
where water has collected on the ledge
which they refrain from using yet
to put out the fire in them.

holding hands in broad daylight

in their joy, in their fire
they hold hands at Wolf Point
and stop on the Riverwalk a while
to catalogue the other's beauty

he traces his heart on the pad of her palm
attracting the attention of strangers who know them
he announces how well he understands
the advance of her breasts beneath his hands
testifying they are no longer neglected

and for the record, he adds
that the thighs of his bride
are awake and burning
now that the war is on

they scale every wall of the streets of the city
and watch themselves from the other side
everyone wants what they have
holding hands in broad daylight
for what counts tonight
is how near they sleep
ignoring every searchlight

later they lie temporarily in ruins
and weave again the tether

to the threads of their vow
not to suffer within their communion

33 the sulphur priest

at dawn he went to the temple seeking dissolution
but the priest's benedictions were mysterious
the indulgences of the Raccolta severe

instead
the clergy rang the moisture
from her femininity
and lashed his back for thirsting

the priest condemned them to a faraway pillory
for want of absolution
and behind the temple curtain
he posted his conviction

you lingered too long
on her thighs
she moved you like some feral vixen

the sinner's head was bowed
no other ever touched me so, he said
like angel dancers from far Babylon

the sulphur priest executed his duty
flicked lit lunts into their faces
setting fire their rose-cheeked beauty

he splayed her swaying waist

on the pinning block
every temple, every sacristy decreed
they shall be formless now and scorned
absent from the other
remedied only by secret sulphur signals
prostrated at the chancel

inside the dark confessional
others knelt and mourned
quietly

when they lie down

they agree before undressing
that mystery holds the stars in line
along the milky way
and concur that fractal fronds and wonder
pull Fundy tides toward the moon

all comparisons in the sky, though
are nameless, rendless, hewn
when they lie down

under him she looks up
with eyes that are morning sun
they both are new inside her

the heads of lovers on every continent turn in unison
to look and learn this love
whole forests are pulled skyward
like rising flocks of doves

he is eager for this sacred duty
his arms fold firmly the tyranny of her beauty
and when his shoulders drop to her
he claims the change from both to one

he is not weary wanting more, incomparably, finally
they know what they have left behind
cured by their learning, an eimi of two

they no longer fear the fallen saints
they possess the soft eyes of sweating satyrid butterflies
weary from flight
but the mercy of their prayer is angelic
their exiled selves infinite and precise

the terms of his surrender

on the last day he knelt to confess
the terms of his surrender
wept privately, not wanting to offend her

their guardian angel overheard him ask
can we dance once more before you go
before we have to go

whence the intimate mercy of your lips
he whispered the question urgently
he pleaded to live beside her

but her case was packed, concluded
I have loved you all the cruel spring long, she wept
and look, we have come through, my friend

he cannot breathe without her
the mark her breasts made on him
will remain a sin til morning
when he will beg all lovers of the world to forgive them
guided by signals in their skin

the keepers of the garden of beloveds
carry off their bodies prone
tie signs around their necks

he forgot to ask for more

a lock of her hair at least
and in the moment of his surrender
no gasp was precise enough
when she passed alone
through the Heathman door

sad proscenium

his hands square a proscenium
of forest and fast river
she moves into the frame
beckoned by the blurred bank opposite
where a little one watches
mama, I'm here
the tiny whisper joining all their words
already set free on the water
skitting the riffles like whirligig beetles

she does not hesitate
bends, pulls the water in around her
swims headlong again
toward the moment of birth
every pull of her arms and slash of her legs
making for the farther shore

in the trees above
another figure gestures
weakly

the name of the beloved

later the same morning he lept from the cliff
where strategic appellations are shaped and timed
in free fall he proclaimed her name
the slide and sound of the vowels and consonants
smooth, sweet and finely sewn to him

she heard her name announced thereafter
in the airports of foreign countries
she heard him mouthing the contours of the diminutive
while she slid segments of Fuyu persimmons
slowly inside her mouth
sitting on the boulevard of their Paris café

he invited her to watch with him
from a balcony in Barcelona
where they stood watching witnesses
assembled in righteous ranks on Rambla Catalunya
scurrying in circles with rigid wills and lances

he put his arms around her from behind
and spoke her name into her hair
she turned and kissed everything she missed before

then her name flew like a moon out to sea
a blue cotton dress caught in a gust
a river beyond his reach

she arced her back to meet his breath
it mattered not a wit to them
what the witnesses made of that

today I died

today I died
she arrived immediately at the porous ceremony
with a eulogy for my demise
announcing that my body was done

when is it ever as easy as that
a dying and a forgetting
she asked the mourning angels
who were present like morning light
sneaking out in front of stars
like fish finning downstream in spring

there came as well to hear her speak
a shadow man arriving for the wake
padded there on clever feet
with my heart dripping red in his pack

when she left, my soul followed furtively
the water and light in our way
healed fast behind our intrusion
a slow elegance of eternal refolding

alert as an officer on the field of fire
my dead eyes fastened on hers
and we remembered the holiness of our happiness

there is wonder and pain, I said
on this precipice, this glowing pyre
where love fire prevails imperially
and softens the carnage of magistrates
who report the flames as unknowable

on the path behind us
every perfect flake of late snow
passes slowly and without protest
on the warming earth of spring

testament in rock

we returned that fall to the place in the pines
where our furtive footprints are mute
enduring inside thin understory

we sat that day against the granite rock
abandoned by retreating ice
I revealed and you heard me say
god let me let you in

we knew that pilgrims centuries hence
would brush traces of the frankincense we breathed
and find your scent and find our tears
which my lungs held in

we prayed for upward shoots of love to stir again
to shoulder up from smothering dull roots
and hidden veins of truth running close to the bone
testament of love locked down
hushed like slow magma

as softly as the weightless passing butterfly
which alighted on the rock where we sat
we held mortal love against our bones
so wounded were we then
that no one could hurt us more
or more
again

eggs in a nest

I was walking back
talking to you in my solitude
and singularity
my heart as hard as flint that day
until I came upon an untended nest
eggs oddly olive, there in the lesser celandine
marked with squiggles in brown and black

reflecting like the fearful monk on the chalice
which Tristan and Isolde did not refuse
and a kingdom wobbled into war thereby
I tried whistling
and startled two terns from the sea
pale grey and white below
they swooped and ascended rapidly
to and from the forest floor

failed witness to their flight
I missed the detail of their wings
and the lessons of their wandering

the perfect courtesy of water

my usual tricks no longer work
my whole life smaller now
a mess by every measure
exhausted hearts cannot hold it all

like the perfect courtesy of water
love let me in
closed around my soul

then you said, perhaps to stay the breaking
the sea will heave, the earth undulate
making and unmaking
the immutable sky and our mad love
tending to their purposes
will ignore our iridescent tears
and the variegated webs of spring
will collapse

the hands of love around our throats again
tighten without apology

you look at me, past me
remembering like a knife blade
us in the pinewood
kissing then

fleeing to Catalonia

her absence is a fist in his belly
the untameable becomes foreboding
an alliance of the condemned for his cell

he moves in on the bruising
kicks out the racket of it
banishes the nameless place in his body
where the memory of touch has lived

he aches to nuzzle every part
to see her seeing him
but blades move like an ouroboros
hemming her endlessly in
and away from him

gone, gone talking all night in the dark
and her shuffling breath
in the household of God

lie, burrow, dissimulate
do whatever it takes, he cries to the east
pass a week in Barcelona with me

I'll buy your ticket, I'll buy you wine
and bring along books from Greenwood too
we'll awake in us all the day long
the heaven of touch to see us through

I'll bring you breakfast in bed, my love
I'll do all this tomorrow
in Catalonia

in the east her mouth is startled
her eyes look inside
at the idea of him

making for the beginning

while masons work on the walls
of our decaying homes
we go to a café by the sea
and by how the light finds our table
we know dim rededication
to allay the slow fade we fled
is cirrus love inside a lie

we make for Catalonia
a church bell on Sunday morning
awakens us in the Pulitzer
our bodies issue reports
of desire ebbing into grief

we flee then to the desert
where in the shade of dark terebinths
we compose sad songs
about all we live without
and wet red silk on skin
and about our particularity

on our way to receive the Holy Spirit
we dare not look back
at the salt lovers we pass

when time runs out

we make for the beginning
but find the table gone
and the sea deeper, colder, brimming

the longing has no proprietor

I write you down like a photograph
and lean each night in the Cathedral door
watching for your picture
signalling from the east

I am a grey chalice heaped appallingly
with those days and nights
when we feared to hear our names aloud

you looked at me for so long
until I stepped behind your eyes
to see my unnamed, exiled self

I saw around your neck like a noose
the resplendent red bandana we used
to wipe back tears of unknown origin

now go I far and high
to chant you privately
in vespers whose intervallic slur
cannot disguise raw secret love
from the watching witnesses

I go regularly to Paris
to live my fantasy
your legs around my body
your eyes inside of me

my body is not yet cleansed
stooping me to sad strategies

soft facts and fractions froth up
immutable
each one just in this moment
incomplete, thoroughly asleep
so inscrutable

the petrel and the fletcher

we dispatched the ancient petrel far to sea
climb fast and high and then descend again, we said
hover as you do above us, circle in the night
one day you will be our beacon
our compass, in high familiar flight

when your vigil is complete
and bidden back we are
to cross the grimpen mire
carry we will our long clenched love
and the wisdom of the fire

the promise of the sonnet in us
will make the journey too
through spaces treacherous
where like taxing stones in a river
there are those who may slow us
or refuse to let us pass
but spring love aimed true by the feathers
of an arrow from the mythic fletcher's quiver
will course fearless over all of that

for are we not conspirators
and is enchantment not our future?

though new witnesses may eschew the petrel's flight

or love as never sin
they will see by our eyes
however vexed to silence we were then
our flesh, our hearts now prove otherwise

meaning, she said to him in endless answering
not yet, dear one
not here, not now

not alone

about the author

David Schleich is the former publisher
and editor of Quarry Press and of *Quarry
Magazine*, one of Canada's oldest literary
periodicals. He is an accomplished inter-
national essayist and a university president.
He lives in Portland, Oregon.

CPSIA information can be obtained
at www.ICGtesting.com
Printed in the USA
LVHW01n0321020218
565013LV00010B/30/P